RONALD
REAGAN

PIVOTAL PRESIDENTS
PROFILES IN LEADERSHIP

RONALD
REAGAN

Edited by Michael Anderson

Britannica®
Educational Publishing
IN ASSOCIATION WITH
ROSEN
EDUCATIONAL SERVICES

Published in 2013 by Britannica Educational Publishing
(a trademark of Encyclopædia Britannica, Inc.) in association with Rosen Educational Services, LLC
29 East 21st Street, New York, NY 10010.

Distributed exclusively by Rosen Educational Services.
For a listing of additional Britannica Educational Publishing titles, call toll free (800) 237-9932.

First Edition

Britannica Educational Publishing
J.E. Luebering: Director, Core Reference Group, Encyclopædia Britannica
Adam Augustyn: Assistant Manager, Encyclopædia Britannica

Anthony L. Green: Editor, Compton's by Britannica
Michael Anderson: Senior Editor, Compton's by Britannica
Andrea R. Field: Senior Editor, Compton's by Britannica
Sherman Hollar: Senior Editor, Compton's by Britannica

Marilyn L. Barton: Senior Coordinator, Production Control
Steven Bosco: Director, Editorial Technologies
Lisa S. Braucher: Senior Producer and Data Editor
Yvette Charboneau: Senior Copy Editor
Kathy Nakamura: Manager, Media Acquisition

Rosen Educational Services
Shalini Saxena: Editor
Nelson Sá: Art Director
Cindy Reiman: Photography Manager
Marty Levick: Photo Researcher
Brian Garvey: Designer, Cover Design
Introduction by Shalini Saxena

Library of Congress Cataloging-in-Publication Data

Ronald Reagan/edited by Michael Anderson.—1st ed.
    p. cm.—(Pivotal presidents: profiles in leadership)
"In association with Britannica Educational Publishing, Rosen Educational Services."
Includes bibliographical references and index.
ISBN 978-1-61530-944-3 (library binding)
1. Reagan, Ronald—Juvenile literature. 2. United States—Politics and government—1981–1989—Juvenile
literature. 3. Presidents—United States—Biography—Juvenile literature. I. Anderson, Michael, 1972–
E877.R656 2013
973.927092--dc23
[B]
                                                                                    2012026713

Manufactured in the United States of America

On the cover, page 3: Behind the portrait of Ronald Reagan is a photograph taken at the Geneva
summit in 1985, where U.S. Pres. Ronald Reagan met for the first time with Soviet Premier Mikhail
Gorbachev. Following the meeting, Soviet foreign minister Eduard Shevardnadze *(seated, left)* and U.S.
Secretary of State George Shultz *(seated, right)* signed an agreement related to arms reductions, while
the respective leaders looked on. *U.S. Department of Defense (Reagan portait); AFP/Getty Images (Geneva
summit).*

Cover, pp. 1, 3 (flag) © iStockphoto.com/spxChrome; pp. 5, 12, 26, 37, 47, 57, 63, 71, 74, 78, 79 Fedorov
Oleksiy/Shutterstock.com

Table of Contents

A statue of Ronald Reagan stands in the Rotunda of the Capitol in Washington, D.C. *Tom Williams/CQ-Roll Call Group/Getty Images*

Imagine for a moment the events of March 30, 1981: Ronald Reagan, the 40th U.S. president, has just been shot and seriously wounded, he is rushed to the hospital, and in the midst of chaos and panic...he cracks a joke, quipping to doctors that he hoped they "were all Republicans" (the party with which Reagan was affiliated). As an actor-turned-governor-turned president, Ronald Reagan was no stranger to maintaining a public face, and it was perhaps his ability to maintain such calm under pressure that endeared him to so much of the country and, fittingly, earned him the nickname the Great Communicator. As with just about every president, Reagan's time in office had both high and low points, but for many Reagan became—and remains—a representation of the American ideal. Reagan's extraordinary journey, from sportscaster to actor, from governor to president, from liberal to conservative, is recounted in the following pages.

Reagan's résumé was a varied one, to say the least, with entries that may not seem typical of a U.S. president; in fact, it may even seem that his political career came as a second act. Taken together, however, the three areas most significant to his life—athletics, drama, and politics—complemented each other, each revealing his ability and confidence in front of others. In college, Reagan indulged these interests, joining the football, swimming, and track teams, participating in productions by the drama club, and serving as president of his freshman class and then the student body.

After college, Reagan focused on a career in media and entertainment, first working as a radio sportscaster and later as an actor. Although he appeared primarily in supporting roles in B movies and on television, Reagan was active in Hollywood, serving as the president of the Screen Actors Guild for six terms. During his tenure, Reagan helped achieve several measures that benefited actors. However, it was also during this time that his anticommunist leanings—which would remain a theme throughout his political career—became evident. He cooperated with the House Un-American Activities Committee, which attempted to eliminate communist influence in Hollywood by blacklisting actors, directors, and writers believed to have ties to communism.

Following this period, Reagan's focus shifted increasingly to politics. He had been a lifelong Democrat like his father, but partly due to the influence of his wife, Nancy, Reagan became more conservative and officially registered as a Republican in 1962. His televised speech in support of Republican presidential candidate Barry Goldwater in 1964 launched him into the national political arena, and by 1966 he had attracted enough support to be elected governor of California.

Despite his successes as governor, Reagan failed in his attempts to win the Republican bid for the presidency in 1968 and 1976. By 1980, though, the political climate was right, and Reagan was elected the 40th U.S. president. His administration faced some major setbacks, including a severe recession and the infamous Iran-Contra scandal, in which arms were illegally sold to Iran in an effort to secure the release of American hostages in Lebanon. However, having overseen a period of economic growth and improved relations with the Soviet Union, Reagan regained much of his popularity by the end of his two terms.

Armed with the charisma of an actor and the confidence of a seasoned politician, Reagan emerged from his humble beginnings to pursue his greatest ambitions, thus fulfilling the promise of the American dream. Even after his passing, Reagan has remained a beacon of the Republican Party. Readers of this volume will learn about the personality and politics that shaped Reagan's legacy and made him the pivotal leader he came to be.

CHAPTER 1

Early Life and Acting Career

In a stunning electoral landslide, Ronald Reagan was elected the 40th president of the United States in 1980. A former actor known for his folksy charm and confident ease as a public speaker, the Great Communicator, as he was sometimes called, won the votes of divergent groups who had not traditionally supported the Republican Party. He defeated Jimmy Carter, the incumbent Democratic president, by an electoral vote of 489 to 49. In 1984 he was reelected with an unprecedented 525 electoral votes.

Reagan was considered to be the most conservative candidate to win the office in half a century. He was a critic of social-welfare programs, an advocate of a strong military, and a zealous opponent of communism. He was also one of the few men to become president who had not spent the major part of his life in politics or in a closely related public service profession. For 30 years he had been primarily an entertainer in radio, motion pictures, and television. Although he had been active in political causes, he did not become a candidate for public office until he was in his mid-50s.

CHILDHOOD AND EDUCATION

Ronald Wilson Reagan was born on Feb. 6, 1911, in Tampico, Ill., a small town in the northwestern part of the state. He was the second of two sons born to John Edward Reagan (called Jack) and Nelle Wilson Reagan. His nickname, Dutch, came from his father's habit of referring to his infant son as his "fat little Dutchman."

Jack Reagan was a Democrat known for his outspoken opposition to racial bigotry. Nelle Reagan, who was more conservative, gave dramatic readings at women's clubs, hospitals, and jails. Jack Reagan was a shoe salesman who moved his family from one small town to another in Illinois, finally

Reagan *(second from right)* with his parents, Jack and Nelle, and his brother, Neil, c. 1915. *Courtesy Ronald Reagan Library*

settling in Dixon, Ill., when Ronald was nine. Jack opened a shoe store with a former boss, but it soon failed. He later held a minor government job distributing relief checks during the Great Depression. Nelle Reagan helped out by working in a dress shop. She taught Ronald how to read at an early age. Although Ronald was slight and nearsighted, he liked athletics. Beginning at age 14, he held part-time and summer jobs. His first job was as a construction laborer. For several years he was a summer lifeguard.

In high school and college Reagan showed his ability in the three fields that came to dominate his life—sports, drama, and politics. At Eureka College in Eureka, Ill., he was a varsity guard on the football team and was captain of the swimming team; he also participated in track. A member of the drama club, he had roles in college dramatic productions. As president of the freshman class he helped organize a student strike against cutbacks in the curriculum, which led to the resignation of the president of the college. Reagan later was president of the student body. Although he earned only passing grades, he graduated in 1932 with a bachelor's degree in economics and sociology.

Ronald Reagan received a partial scholarship to play football at Eureka College. *Courtesy Ronald Reagan Library*

RADIO, MOVIES, AND TELEVISION

Trying to launch a career in show business, Reagan auditioned for radio station WOC in Davenport, Iowa, by improvising play-by-play commentary for a football game. He was hired to announce the University of Iowa football games for $10 a game, and by the end of 1932 he became a staff announcer.

The next year Reagan was transferred to an affiliated station, WHO, in Des Moines. An announcer there until 1937, he also wrote a sports column for a newspaper. Among his duties was broadcasting Chicago Cubs baseball games. Because the station could not afford to send him to Wrigley Field in Chicago, Reagan was forced to improvise a running account of the games based on sketchy details delivered over a teletype machine.

While at the Cubs training camp in California in 1937, Reagan took a screen test for the Warner Brothers studio. He was signed to a contract at $200 a week. During the following 27 years he appeared in more than 50 movies. In his first movie, *Love Is on the Air*, Reagan played a radio announcer. Throughout his career he most often had supporting roles, frequently as the sidekick of the hero. In only his last film, *The Killers*, was Reagan cast as a villain. Among his best-known movies were *Brother Rat*, *Dark Victory*, *Knute Rockne— All American* (in which his role as George Gipp earned him the lifelong nickname "the Gipper"), and *King's Row*.

While filming *Brother Rat* in 1938, Reagan met Jane Wyman, another Warners contract player. Married in 1940, they had a daughter, Maureen Elizabeth, in 1941; in 1945 they adopted a son, Michael Edward. They divorced in 1948.

During World War II Reagan was a member of the Army Air Corps, but he was rejected for active duty because of his poor eyesight. He spent the war years narrating training films and was discharged with the rank of captain in 1945.

Reagan served six terms—from 1947 to 1952 and in 1959–60—as president of the Screen Actors Guild, the union of movie actors. He helped achieve better pay, revised tax procedures, and improved working conditions for actors. Beginning in 1949, Reagan served two terms as chairman of the Motion Picture Industry Council.

Militantly anticommunist, Reagan appeared in 1947 as a cooperative witness

Reagan ice skating with his first wife, actress Jane Wyman, c. 1945. *Archive Photos/Getty Images* before the House Committee on Un-American Activities, which was investigating communist influence in the movie industry. He cooperated with the movie studios' infamous policy of blacklisting, or refusing to employ actors, directors, and writers suspected of having communist sympathies.

In 1952 Reagan married the actress Nancy Davis. In 1957 the couple appeared together

A poster advertising *Hellcats of the Navy*, a film starring both Reagan and his second wife, Nancy Davis. This was the only film in which the couple appeared together. *Courtesy Ronald Reagan Library*

in the war movie *Hellcats of the Navy*. The Reagans had a large ranch where they raised horses and cattle.

After having performed on several television programs, in 1954 Reagan began an eight-year association with the General Electric Company. He was the host and

Ronald Reagan hosted the television series *General Electric Theater* from 1954 to 1962. *Courtesy Ronald Reagan Library*

program supervisor for the popular television series *General Electric Theater*, and he occasionally appeared as an actor in the series. As part of his contract, Reagan also spent several weeks each year speaking to General Electric employees throughout the country. During these talks he frequently defended free enterprise and criticized big government. Eventually his speeches became too controversial for the company's taste, and he was fired as both spokesman and television host in 1962. Between 1964 and 1966 Reagan hosted and occasionally acted in the *Death Valley Days* series.

Nancy Reagan

When Ronald Reagan became the 40th president of the United States in 1981, it was generally agreed that his wife, Nancy, was one of his most trusted advisers. While some people admired the way the first lady took care of her husband and shared in his career, others thought she exerted too much behind-the-scenes influence. Her tenure as first lady was filled with such mixed reviews on many fronts, ranging from the causes she chose to support to the glamorous clothes she wore.

She was born Anne Frances Robbins in New York City on July 6, 1921, but was nicknamed Nancy as an infant. Following her parents' separation, Nancy spent most of her early childhood in the care of an aunt and uncle while her mother, Edith Luckett Robbins, resumed an acting career. In 1929, when her mother married Loyal Davis, a wealthy Chicago neurosurgeon, Nancy went to live with the couple. Davis eventually adopted Nancy, and she assumed his last name.

Ronald Reagan visits his wife, Nancy, on the set of her movie *Donovan's Brain* in 1953. *Courtesy Ronald Reagan Library*

After graduation from the Chicago Latin School for Girls, Nancy enrolled at all-female Smith College in Northampton, Mass., where she majored in drama. After graduation in 1943, her mother's theater friends helped Nancy obtain a job with a touring company and then a role on Broadway. By 1949 she was working in Hollywood, and she eventually made 11 movies, including *East Side, West Side* (1949), *Shadow on the Wall* (1950), and *Hellcats of the Navy* (1957), in which she starred with Reagan.

Nancy met Reagan in California in 1951, and they married in 1952. Their daughter Patricia Ann (Patti) was born in October, and their son Ronald Prescott in 1958; Reagan was already the father of a daughter, Maureen, and had adopted a son, Michael, with his first wife, actress Jane Wyman.

Many people credited the influence of Nancy and her stepfather for Reagan's progressive shift to the right in the 1950s and his switch to the Republican Party in 1962. He launched his political career in 1966, winning election as governor of California. During her eight years as the governor's wife, Nancy developed skills that later served her in the White House, but she also aroused controversy. She was criticized for her circle of wealthy, glamorous friends; her expensive, stylish outfits; and her insistence on renting a beautiful house in Sacramento rather than living in the governor's mansion.

Nancy often said that she admired the style and elegance of former first lady Jacqueline Kennedy, and she hired Letitia Baldrige, a Kennedy staff member, to assist her at the White House. Designer dresses and costly caviar replaced the more modest attire and fare of her predecessor, Rosalynn Carter, and the guest list included many Hollywood celebrities.

Criticism of the first lady's extravagance led advisers to suggest that she play down her contacts with celebrities and associate herself with a serious cause, prompting her to begin the anti-drug campaign "Just Say No." In an effort to win over critical journalists, she appeared at a Gridiron dinner in March 1982 wearing old, unattractive clothing and sang about her "secondhand" clothes. After that event, her press coverage became more positive and her popularity rose.

Despite her protests, the view persisted that the first lady influenced her husband in personnel matters and on important issues such as arms control and relations with the Soviet Union. When television cameras caught her whispering answers to reporters' questions in the president's ear, speculation increased about her role.

The Reagans left the White House in January 1989, returning to their estate in California, and Nancy continued her anti-drug work under the auspices of the Nancy Reagan Foundation. That same year she published the book *My Turn*, in which she gave her own account of her life in the White House. After her husband was diagnosed with Alzheimer's disease in 1994, she devoted all her time to caring for him and made very few political appearances.

CHAPTER 2

State and National Politics

During the 1930s and '40s Reagan was a liberal Democrat and a member of liberal political organizations, including the United World Federalists and the Americans for Democratic Action. He greatly admired Franklin D. Roosevelt, and in 1948 he supported President Harry S. Truman for reelection. But his political opinions gradually grew more conservative. After first supporting Democratic senatorial candidate Helen Douglas in 1950, he switched his allegiance to Republican Richard Nixon midway through the campaign. Although he was still a Democrat, Reagan worked for Dwight D. Eisenhower in the presidential campaigns of 1952 and 1956, and in 1960 he backed Nixon. In 1962 he officially switched his registration to the Republican Party and also supported a

Reagan *(center right)* leads a rally of Goldwater supporters outside of the Cow Palace in San Francisco, Calif., in 1964. ©*AP Images*

member of the right-wing John Birch Society in an unsuccessful congressional bid.

In 1964 Reagan supported Senator Barry Goldwater, a conservative Republican candidate for president. His televised appeal for Goldwater was the most successful fund-raising political speech in history. It catapulted Reagan onto the national political stage.

GOVERNORSHIP OF CALIFORNIA

With the support of businessmen and other conservative backers Reagan entered the 1966 race for the governorship of California. The incumbent, Democrat Edmund G. (Pat) Brown, ridiculed Reagan's lack of experience, declaring that while he (Brown) had been serving the public, Reagan was making *Bedtime for Bonzo*, a 1951 movie in which Reagan starred with a chimpanzee. But Reagan turned this apparent liability into an asset by portraying himself as an ordinary citizen who was fed up with a state government that had become inefficient and unaccountable. The public also reacted well to Reagan's personality, in particular to his apparent genuineness, affability, and self-deprecating sense of humor. (When asked by a reporter how he would perform in office, Reagan replied, "I don't know. I've never played a governor.") Although registered Democrats outnumbered Republicans by three to two in the state, Reagan won by nearly a million votes. He was reelected in 1970.

As governor of California, Reagan was not wholly successful in carrying out his conservative programs. During his two terms the state had its largest budget increases in history and spending nearly doubled. Partly because of previous deficits, Reagan

Associate Justice Marshall McComb *(center)*, associate justice of the California Supreme Court, swears in Reagan in as governor of California in 1967. Reagan's son, Ronald Prescott, looks on, while Nancy Reagan stands in the rear *(left)*. *Courtesy Ronald Reagan Library*

increased taxes at a rate greater than the national average, and taxes became more progressive. California voters rejected his proposal to limit state spending and levels of taxation. Reagan did, however, accomplish some of his goals. He vetoed 994 bills passed by the state legislature, and all but one of the vetoes were upheld.

Several of Reagan's accomplishments during his terms as governor were highly regarded, even by his political opponents. He doubled aid to schools and increased expenditures for mental health by 400 percent. He cooperated with the legislature in reforming the state's welfare system by restricting eligibility and reducing the number of people receiving benefits, while increasing benefits for the most needy. Reagan also signed the most stringent air and water pollution bills in the country and promoted judicial reform.

PRESIDENTIAL AMBITIONS

In 1968, while serving his first term as governor of California, Reagan announced his candidacy for president during the Republican convention. As a conservative alternative to Nixon, who was the front-runner, Reagan

Reagan, with wife Nancy at his side, meets with supporters at a campaign stop in Rhode Island during his run for president in 1976. © *AP Images*

received only 14 percent of the delegate votes, and Nixon was nominated. Reagan's disagreement with the foreign policy of Nixon's successor, President Gerald R. Ford, led him to enter the 1976 race for the Republican nomination. Reagan defeated Ford in several primaries, but he did not enter primaries in enough large states to win a clear majority of the delegates. Reagan lost the nomination to Ford by only 117 delegate votes.

In 1979 Reagan again entered the race for the Republican presidential nomination.

This time he dominated the party's primary elections. Although his strongest opponent, George H.W. Bush, won an upset victory in the Iowa caucuses, Reagan bounced back after a notable performance in a debate with other Republican candidates in Nashua, N.H. The debate, initially sponsored by a newspaper, was first extended to only Reagan and Bush, but Reagan decided to pay for the debate and invited the rest of the candidates. When all the candidates took the stage that evening, the Bush team appeared surprised, and, as Reagan began to explain the situation, the moderator from the newspaper instructed that Reagan's microphone be turned off. Reagan responded memorably with an angry line he remembered from a Spencer Tracy movie: "I am paying for this microphone!"

Reagan went on to win New Hampshire and most of the other major primaries and entered the Republican National Convention in July 1980 with a commanding lead. He won the nomination on the first ballot with 1,939 votes to 37 for John Anderson and 13 for Bush, who had withdrawn from the contest before the vote. Reagan chose Bush as his running mate.

ELECTION OF 1980

The Republican platform for the presidential election was tailored to suit Reagan's views. It advocated large tax cuts, decreased government spending for social programs, increased military spending, and a more aggressive foreign policy.

Reagan's opponent was Jimmy Carter, the Democratic incumbent president. Carter began the campaign in a vulnerable position. Inflation had doubled since his first year in office, and unemployment and interest rates were also high. An even more important factor than the economy, however, was Carter's apparent inability to resolve the Iran hostage crisis, which had continued for almost a year at the time of the election. On Nov. 4, 1979, a mob of Iranian students had stormed the U.S. embassy in Tehran and taken the diplomatic staff there hostage. In April 1980, after months of fruitless negotiations

A campaign button from Reagan's 1980 presidential campaign features an image of Reagan (left) and vice-presidential candidate George H.W. Bush as well as Reagan's campaign slogan. *Fotosearch/Archive Photos/Getty Images*

A blindfolded American hostage stands among Iranian demonstrators at the U.S. embassy in Tehran. *Alain Mingam/Gamma-Rapho/Getty Images*

with students and officials of Iran's revolutionary government (which had sanctioned the takeover), Carter ordered a military rescue operation, which failed dramatically. The hostage crisis contributed to a general public perception of the Carter administration as weak and indecisive, and the failed rescue mission reinforced Reagan's charge that the Democrats had allowed the country's military to deteriorate badly.

After the nominating convention Reagan lost the large lead he had held over Carter, and the candidates were often tied in the polls.

Reagan *(right)* stands with his vice-presidential candidate, George H.W. Bush, at the Republican National Convention in Detroit, Mich., in 1980. *Dirk Halstead/Getty Images*

Even though Reagan was often criticized for not being specific, his ability as a speaker helped him project a favorable image. His strong performance in a debate with Carter one week before the election was credited with winning over a large number of voters. During the debate Reagan memorably reminded his national television audience of the country's economic problems by asking, "Are you better off now than you were four years ago?"

On election day Reagan defeated Carter and John Anderson (who ran as an independent) with slightly more than half the popular vote, against Carter's 41 percent and Anderson's 7 percent. The vote in the electoral college was 489 to Carter's 49. At age 69, Reagan was the oldest person to be elected president.

CHAPTER 3

Reagan's Domestic Policies

From the beginning of his presidency Reagan tried to reduce the role of the federal government. His administration set a new tone, indicated in such themes as "getting the government off the backs of the people" and not letting it spend more than it takes in.

FIRST DAYS

Reagan's presidency began on a dramatic note when, after the inaugural ceremony, he announced at a luncheon that Iran had agreed to release the remaining American hostages. The timing of Iran's decision led to suspicions, which were never substantiated, that the Reagan campaign had made a secret

Ronald and Nancy Reagan wave to crowds on the day of his first inauguration as president, Jan. 20, 1981. *Courtesy Ronald Reagan Library*

deal with the Iranians to prevent the Carter administration from unveiling a so-called "October surprise"—the release of the hostages in October 1980, before election day.

Then, on March 30, 1981, a deranged drifter named John W. Hinckley, Jr., fired six shots at Reagan as he left a Washington, D.C., hotel. One of the bullets entered Reagan's chest, puncturing a lung and lodging one inch from his heart. Rushed to the hospital for emergency surgery, Reagan joked with doctors as he was being wheeled into the operating

Nancy Reagan with her husband at George Washington University Hospital, where he was recovering from the assassination attempt of March 30, 1981. ©*AP Images* room: "I hope you're all Republicans." After his release 12 days later, Reagan made a series of carefully staged public appearances designed to give the impression that he was recovering quickly, though in fact he remained seriously weakened for months and his workload was sharply reduced.

In August 1981, 13,000 members of the national union of air traffic controllers, the Professional Air Traffic Controllers Organization (PATCO) walked off their jobs, demanding higher pay and better working conditions. As federal employees, the PATCO members were forbidden by law to strike, and Reagan refused to negotiate, giving them 48 hours to return to work. Most of the striking controllers ignored the ultimatum and were promptly fired. Although the firings caused delays and reductions in air traffic until replacements were hired and trained, the public generally reacted positively to Reagan's action, seeing it as a sign of decisiveness and conviction.

ECONOMIC POLICY

Following the so-called "supply-side" economic program put forth in his campaign, Reagan proposed massive tax cuts—30

Presidents *(left to right)* Ronald Reagan, Gerald Ford, Jimmy Carter, and Richard Nixon, 1982. *U.S. Department of Defense*

percent reductions in both individual and corporate income taxes over a three-year period. He believed that the cuts would stimulate the economy and eventually increase revenues from taxes as income levels grew. At the same time, he proposed large increases

Supply-side Economics

Reagan was a firm believer in supply-side economics. This theory holds that reductions in federal taxes on businesses and individuals lead to increased economic growth and in the long run to increased government revenue. It was put forth in the 1970s by the U.S. economist Arthur Laffer and implemented by Reagan during his presidency. Supporters point to the economic growth of the 1980s as proof of its effectiveness. Critics point out the massive federal deficits and speculation that went along with that growth.

The supply-side economic theories of Arthur Laffer strongly influenced Reagan's economic policies. ©*AP Images*

in military spending and significant cuts in spending on social-welfare programs such as education, food stamps, and low-income housing. In 1981 Congress passed most of the president's budget proposals.

A severe recession in 1982 lessened the appeal of so-called Reaganomics. The country's unemployment rate climbed to nearly 11 percent, the highest it had been since the Great Depression of the 1930s. Bankruptcies and farm foreclosures reached record levels. The country's trade deficit increased from $25 billion in 1980 to $111 billion in 1984. In addition, the huge increases in military spending, combined with insufficient cuts in other programs, produced the largest budget deficits in the country's history. By the end of Reagan's second term, the deficits would contribute to a tripling of the national debt, to more than $2.5 trillion. To address the deficit problem, Reagan made a policy reversal and supported a tax increase in 1982.

By early 1983 the economy had begun to recover, and by the end of that year unemployment and inflation were significantly reduced. Economic growth continued through the remainder of Reagan's presidency. Critics charged, however, that the tax cuts and the fruits of economic growth benefited mainly the wealthy and that the gap between rich and poor had grown wider.

GOVERNMENT CUTBACKS

In keeping with his aim of reducing the role of government in the country's economy, Reagan cut the budgets of many government departments. He also relaxed or ignored the enforcement of laws and regulations administered by the Environmental Protection Agency (EPA), the Department of the Interior, the Department of Transportation, and the Civil Rights Division of the Department of Justice, among other agencies. After the administration and Congress reduced regulations governing the savings and loan industry in the early 1980s, many savings institutions expanded recklessly through the decade and eventually collapsed, requiring bailouts by the federal government that cost taxpayers some $500 billion.

SUPREME COURT NOMINATIONS

During his presidency Reagan appointed three justices to the Supreme Court. They

Sandra Day O'Connor stands in front of the U.S. Supreme Court. Appointed as a Supreme Court justice in 1981, the first woman to hold that position. *David Hume Kennerly/Getty Images* were Sandra Day O'Connor, the first woman justice; Antonin Scalia; and Anthony Kennedy. He also elevated William Rehnquist to chief justice in 1986 upon the retirement of Warren Burger.

CHAPTER 4

Foreign Affairs in the Reagan Years

When he entered office in 1980, Reagan believed that the United States had grown weak militarily and had lost the respect it once commanded in world affairs. Aiming to restore the country to a position of moral as well as military preeminence in the world, he called for massive increases in the defense budget to expand and modernize the military. He also urged a more aggressive approach to combating communism and related forms of leftist totalitarianism.

RELATIONS WITH THE SOVIET UNION

Reagan took an early stand against the Soviet Union. At his first press conference as president, he boldly questioned the legitimacy of the Soviet government. Two years later, in a memorable speech in Florida, he denounced the Soviet Union as "an evil empire." The behavior of the Soviet Union itself also strained relations between the two superpowers. One incident took place in September 1983 when the Soviets shot down a Korean airliner en route from Alaska to Seoul as it strayed over Soviet territory. All 269 people aboard were killed, including 61 Americans. Reagan's massive military spending program, the largest in American peacetime history, was another factor in the worsening of U.S.-Soviet relations.

STRATEGIC DEFENSE INITIATIVE

A significant component of Reagan's military buildup was his 1983 proposal for a space-based missile defense system that would use lasers and other as-yet-undeveloped technologies to destroy incoming Soviet nuclear missiles before they could reach their targets in the United States. The Strategic Defense Initiative (SDI), popularly called "Star Wars" after the popular science-fiction movie of the late 1970s, was denounced by the Soviets as a dangerous escalation of the arms race. Other critics argued that the project was technologically impossible.

President Reagan *(left)* awards Edward Teller the National Medal of Science in 1983. Teller was a prominent nuclear physicist who greatly influenced Reagan's Strategic Defense Initiative. *Lawrence Livermore National Laboratory (LLNL)*

In later years, however, former Soviet officials cited SDI as a factor in the eventual collapse of their country. They said it showed that the Soviet Union was politically unprepared for and economically incapable of competing in a new arms race with the United States. Although Reagan never abandoned his support for SDI, it was eventually reconceived as a much smaller and more conventional defense system than the one he originally proposed.

Reagan *(center, left)* shakes the hand of Soviet leader Mikhail Gorbachev at the Reykjavík summit in Iceland in 1985. ©*AP Images*

SUMMITS

U.S.-Soviet relations improved considerably during Reagan's second term, not least because Reagan softened his anticommunist rhetoric and adopted a more encouraging tone toward the changes then taking place in the Soviet Union. Reagan and Soviet leader Mikhail Gorbachev met for the first time in November 1985, in Geneva, Switzerland, to discuss reductions in nuclear weapons. At a dramatic summit meeting in Reykjavík, Iceland, in October 1986, Gorbachev proposed a 50 percent reduction in the nuclear

Reagan's Berlin Wall Speech

The Berlin Wall, built by East Germany's Soviet-backed government in 1961, divided the German city of Berlin in half. It separated West Berlin, which was part of democratic West Germany, from East Berlin, the capital of communist East Germany. The wall came to symbolize the Cold War's division of eastern and western Europe. On June 12, 1987, Reagan delivered one of the most famous speeches of his presidency at the Brandenburg Gate of

Reagan delivers his famous address at the Brandenburg Gate in Berlin in 1987. *AFP/Getty Images*

the Berlin Wall, issuing a direct challenge to Soviet leader Mikhail Gorbachev:

General Secretary Gorbachev, if you seek peace, if you seek prosperity for the Soviet Union and eastern Europe, if you seek liberalization: Come here to this gate! Mr. Gorbachev, open this gate! Mr. Gorbachev, tear down this wall!

The communist government of East Germany would fall about two years later, in October 1989. The Berlin Wall was opened the next month.

arsenals of each side, and for a time it seemed as though a historic agreement would be reached. Although the summit ended in failure owing to differences over SDI, it was followed up in December 1987 by a treaty eliminating intermediate-range nuclear forces (INF) on European soil. The INF Treaty was the first arms-control pact to eliminate an entire category of weapon systems.

MIDDLE EAST AND CENTRAL AMERICA

Reagan's strong anticommunist stance also dictated U.S. policy in other parts of the world. He sent U.S. forces to the Caribbean island country of Grenada to depose a leftist regime. He authorized other interventions against communist influence elsewhere, particularly in Latin America. The United States also became entangled in conflicts in Lebanon and Libya during Reagan's presidency.

LEBANON

Following Israel's invasion of Lebanon in June 1982, Reagan sent 800 Marines to join an international force to oversee the evacuation of Palestinian guerrillas from West Beirut, then surrounded by Israeli troops. After Israel withdrew its troops from the Beirut area in September 1983, the Marines remained— along with forces from Italy, France, and Britain—to protect the fragile Lebanese government. This identified the Marines with one of the factions in Lebanon's long and bloody civil war, which had begun in 1975.

On the morning of Oct. 23, 1983, a suicide bomber drove a truck loaded with explosives into the Marine compound at the Beirut airport, killing 241 Marines and wounding 100 others. Although later investigations blamed the Marine chain of command for poor security at the base and "serious errors in judgment," Reagan accepted full blame

The U.S. Marine compound in Beirut, Lebanon, lies in ruins after a truck full of explosives destroyed it and killed 241 Marines. ©*AP Images* for the tragedy himself. He withdrew the Marines from Lebanon in February 1984.

GRENADA

Meanwhile, in Grenada, the prime minister was overthrown and executed in a coup by radical leftists. Less than a week later, and only one day after the bombing of the Marine compound in Lebanon, Reagan ordered an invasion of the country. He justified the action as necessary to prevent Grenada from becoming a dangerous Soviet outpost and to protect American students at the medical school there. Joined by troops from neighboring Caribbean countries, U.S. forces quickly ousted the coup leaders. However, critics charged that the administration had staged the invasion to divert public attention from the bombing in Lebanon.

LIBYA

In January 1986 Reagan imposed economic sanctions on Libya, charging its government with sponsoring acts of international terrorism. In March Libya fired antiaircraft missiles at U.S. warplanes, and the United States responded with attacks on Libyan ships and missile installations. Then, on April 5, two people, including a U.S. serviceman, were killed by a bomb explosion in a discotheque in West Berlin, Germany. Blaming Libya, the United States carried out retaliatory bombing raids on "terrorist-related targets" in Libya.

ANTICOMMUNIST EFFORTS IN LATIN AMERICA

In keeping with Reagan's belief that the United States should do more to prevent the spread of communism, his administration expanded military and economic assistance to governments battling leftist rebellions; conversely, in countries with leftist governments, he supported opposition forces. This policy, which became known as the Reagan Doctrine, was applied most often in Latin America. During the 1980s the United States supported military-dominated governments in El Salvador in a civil war with left-wing guerrilla forces. In Nicaragua the United States backed guerrillas known as Contras in their war against the leftist Sandinista government.

CHAPTER 5

The Iran-Contra Affair

At the time of the presidential election of 1984, Reagan was at the height of his popularity. Using slogans such as "It's morning in America" and "America is back," his reelection campaign emphasized the country's economic prosperity and its renewed leadership role in world affairs. On election day Reagan defeated his Democratic opponent, Walter Mondale, in a landslide of historic proportions.

With most of the country behind him, Reagan's prospects in his second term appeared bright. Only two years later, however, he would become embroiled in the worst scandal of his political career, one that would cost him much popular and party support and significantly impair his ability to lead the country.

ELECTION OF 1984

Reagan (Republican) 525 electoral votes
Mondale (Democratic) 13 electoral votes

© 2009 Encyclopædia Britannica, Inc.

Results of the U.S. presidential election, 1984.

ARMS-FOR-HOSTAGES DEAL

In November 1985, at the suggestion of the head of the National Security Council (NSC), William (Bud) McFarlane, Reagan authorized a secret plan to sell weapons to Iran in exchange for its help in securing the release of American hostages by terrorists in Lebanon. This directly violated the administration's policy of refusing to negotiate with terrorists or to aid countries—such as Iran—that supported terrorism.

Election of 1984

The presidential election of 1984 pitted Reagan against Walter Mondale, who had served as vice president under Jimmy Carter. Mondale struggled from the start to dent Reagan's soaring approval ratings. A brief upward blip in Mondale's fortunes came when, in the first of two nationally televised debates, Reagan appeared tired and confused. His performance brought into the open the issue of Reagan's age (73), and for a short time the Democrats took

Reagan *(right)* debates Walter Mondale, the Democratic candidate in the 1984 presidential campaign, in Louisville, Ky. ©*AP Images*

heart. By the second debate, however, the president was back in command. At that debate Reagan was asked about being the oldest president in U.S. history and whether there was any doubt he could do the job. Reagan disarmingly responded, saying:

I want you to know that also I will not make age an issue of this campaign. I am not going to exploit for political purposes my opponent's youth and inexperience.

Laughter—including from Mondale—ensued. With that statement, age became a nonissue, and Democrats saw little hope of stopping Reagan. His campaign capitalized on the new mood of national pride that had reached a peak in the Los Angeles Olympic Games, with Reagan representing leadership, patriotism, and optimism. Reagan easily defeated Mondale by 59 percent to 41 percent of the popular vote. In the electoral college Reagan received 525 votes to Mondale's 13, the largest number of electoral votes of any candidate in history.

News of the arms-for-hostages deal, first made public in November 1986, proved very embarrassing to the president. Even more damaging, however, was the revelation later that month that profits from the sales had been illegally diverted to the Contras in Nicaragua. The diversion was undertaken by an obscure NSC aide, U.S. Marine Corps Lieutenant Colonel Oliver North, with the

President Reagan delivers the State of the Union address to Congress on Jan. 25, 1984. *Courtesy Ronald Reagan Library*

approval of McFarlane's successor at the NSC, Rear Admiral John Poindexter.

AFTERMATH

In response to the crisis, by this time known as the Iran-Contra Affair, Reagan fired both North and Poindexter and appointed a special commission to investigate the matter. An independent counsel, Judge Lawrence Walsh, was also appointed, and the House and Senate began joint hearings to examine both the arms sales and the military assistance to the Contras. As a result of Walsh's investigations, North and Poindexter were

Lieutenant Colonel Oliver North testifies before Congress about the Iran-Contra Affair. *Consolidated News Pictures/Archive Photos/Getty Images*

convicted on charges of obstructing justice and related offenses, but their convictions were overturned on appeal.

Reagan accepted responsibility for the arms-for-hostages deal but denied any knowledge of the diversion of profits to the Contras. Although no evidence came to light to indicate that he was more deeply involved, many in Congress and the public remained skeptical. Nevertheless, most of the public eventually appeared willing to forgive him for whatever they thought he had done. His popularity, which had dropped dramatically during the first months of the crisis, gradually recovered.

CHAPTER 6

Retirement

In the presidential election of 1988, Reagan campaigned actively for the Republican nominee, Vice President Bush. In large part because of Reagan's continued popularity, Bush defeated Democratic candidate Michael Dukakis.

Neither the many political scandals of his administration nor the weight of enormous budget deficits clung to Reagan. He retired on a crest of popularity to his home in California, where he wrote his autobiography, *An American Life* (1990). President Bush awarded Reagan the Presidential Medal of Freedom, the country's highest civilian honor, in 1993.

Reagan holds up a sign supporting George H.W. Bush at a Bush campaign rally in Little Rock, Ark., in 1988. Congressman John Paul Hammerschmidt stands to the right. ©*AP Images*

DECLINING HEALTH

In 1994, in a letter to the American people, Reagan revealed that he had been diagnosed with Alzheimer's disease, a brain disorder. To some observers Reagan's declining health had been evident for many years. Mindful of her husband's diminished abilities, Nancy Reagan occasionally would screen him from the press by intercepting reporters' questions and then whispering a response in his ear. Reagan's health problems made public appearances difficult for the former

Reagan rides his horse El Alamein at his Santa Barbara ranch in 1985. After his presidency ended in 1989, Reagan retired to his beloved ranch. *Courtesy Ronald Reagan Library*

Alzheimer's Disease

The brain disorder that affected Reagan in his later years was first described in 1906 by German doctor Alois Alzheimer. The symptoms of Alzheimer's disease were long dismissed as normal consequences of human aging, but in the 1980s it came to be recognized as the most common cause of intellectual deterioration in the middle-aged and the elderly. It is characterized by the death of nerve cells in the cerebral cortex—a part of the brain involved in complex functions. The disease's effects—most notably, speech disturbances, disorientation, and severe short-term memory loss—lead to the progressive loss of mental faculties, even though the victim often remains physically healthy.

Alzheimer's disease is the largest single cause of an advanced degree of brain impairment known as senile dementia and is also the major cause of presenile dementia, or dementia not associated with advanced age. An estimated 35.6 million people worldwide were living with dementia in 2010, and that figure was expected to double over the course of the next two decades.

president, but his wife occasionally appeared on his behalf.

FINAL YEARS

In 1991 the Ronald Reagan Presidential Library and Museum was dedicated in Simi

Nancy and Ronald Reagan celebrate his 83rd birthday at a dinner in Washington, D.C., in February 1994. The dinner marked his last speech before he revealed to the public later that year that he had been diagnosed with Alzheimer's disease. ©*AP Images*

Valley, Calif. The institution documents Reagan's historic presidency through an extensive collection of papers, speeches, photographs, and audio and video recordings.

In February 1998 Reagan was honored again when Congress and President Bill Clinton changed the name of National Airport in Washington, D.C., to Ronald Reagan Washington National Airport. Reagan's conservative policies and heated rhetoric had always infuriated liberals, and

Presidents *(left to right)* George H.W. Bush, Ronald Reagan, Jimmy Carter, Gerald Ford, and Richard Nixon attend the opening of the Ronald Reagan Presidential Library in Simi Valley, Calif. in 1991. *Marcy Nighswander—Associated Press/U.S. Department of Defense* his administration had experienced its share of scandals and disappointments. But to his millions of fans and political admirers, this tribute was the least the government could do for the man who had helped to end the Cold War and restored, however fleetingly, the country's confidence in itself and its faith in a better tomorrow.

Reagan died in Los Angeles, Calif., on June 5, 2004, at the age of 93. Following a state funeral in Washington, he was buried at his presidential library in California.

CONCLUSION

In the decades following his presidency, Reagan remained a touchstone for the Republican Party. Politicians looking to bolster their standing among conservatives often compared themselves to the former president, voicing their support for his program of low taxes, limited government involvement in the economy, and a strong military. Beyond these policy matters, however, Republicans have tried to tap into the deep feelings of national pride that Reagan inspired for so many Americans. The frequent appeals to patriotism by 21st-century Republicans can be seen as an attempt to recapture the spirit of Reagan's presidency.

Glossary

bailout A rescue from financial distress.

bankruptcy The status of a debtor who has been declared by judicial process to be unable to pay his or her debts.

blacklist To place a name on a list of persons who are disapproved of or are to be punished or boycotted.

communism A political and economic system in which the major productive resources in a society—such as mines, factories, and farms—are owned by the public or the state, and wealth is divided among citizens equally or according to individual need.

deficit An excess of expenditure over revenue.

dementia A usually progressive condition (as Alzheimer's disease) marked by deteriorated cognitive functioning often with emotional apathy.

foreclosure A legal proceeding by which a mortgagor's (borrower's) rights to a mortgaged property may be extinguished if the mortgagor fails to live up to the obligations agreed to in the mortgage.

Great Depression Worldwide economic downturn that began in 1929 and lasted until about 1939. It was the longest and most severe depression ever experienced by the industrialized Western world, sparking fundamental changes in economic institutions, macroeconomic policy, and economic theory.

inflation A continuing rise in the general price level usually attributed to an increase in the volume of money and credit relative to available goods and services.

intermediate-range nuclear forces (INF) Class of nuclear weapons with a range of 620–3,400 miles (1,000–5,500 kilometers).

social-welfare program Any of a variety of governmental programs designed to protect citizens from economic risks and insecurities, including but not limited to benefits to the elderly or retired, the sick or invalid, dependent survivors, mothers, the unemployed, the work-injured, and families.

speculation The assumption of unusual business risk in hopes of obtaining proportionate gain.

supply-side economics An economic theory that focuses on influencing the supply of labor and goods, using tax cuts and benefit cuts as incentives to work and produce goods.

teletype machine Any of various telegraphic instruments that transmit and receive printed messages and data via telephone cables or radio relay systems.

totalitarianism A form of government that theoretically permits no individual freedom and that seeks to subordinate all aspects of the individual's life to the authority of the government.

union An association of laborers in a particular trade, industry, or company, created for the purpose of securing improvements in pay, benefits, working conditions, or social and political status through collective bargaining.

For More Information

American Historical Association (AHA)
400 A Street SE
Washington, DC 20003
(202) 544-2422
Web site: http://www.historians.org
The AHA serves as a leader and advocate for professionals, researchers, and students in the field of history and upholds academic and professional standards. The AHA also awards a number of fellowships and prizes and offers resources and publications for anyone interested in the field.

Miller Center
2201 Old Ivy Road
Charlottesville, VA 22904
(434) 924-7236
Web site: http://millercenter.org

The Miller Center at the University of
Virginia furthers understanding of the
presidency, political history, and policy
through its various research initia-
tives, programs, events, and fellowship
opportunities.

National Museum of American History
(NMAH)
1400 Constitution Avenue NW
Washington, DC 20560
(202) 633-1000
Web site: http://americanhistory.si.edu
With more than 3 million artifacts of
American history in its collection, many
of which are on display, the NMAH is
dedicated to promoting public interest
in the events that shaped the American
nation. Its "The American Presidency:
A Glorious Burden" exhibit profiles U.S.
presidents through collections of their
personal belongings, campaign memora-
bilia, and many other items.

Ronald Reagan Boyhood Home
816 South Hennepin Avenue
Dixon, IL 61021
(815) 288-5176

Web site: http://reaganhome.org
Restored and outfitted with furnishings
typical of the era, the Ronald Reagan
Boyhood Home allows visitors to tour
the house where the 40th U.S. president
lived with his family from 1920 until 1923
and to learn lesser-known stories of his
childhood.

Ronald Reagan Presidential Foundation and
Library
40 Presidential Drive
Simi Valley, CA 93065
(800) 410-8354
Web site: http://www.reaganfoundation.org
With a collection that includes a piece of
the Berlin Wall and the Air Force One
plane used by Ronald Reagan during
his time as president, as well as interac-
tive exhibits chronicling the milestones
of Reagan's career, the Ronald Reagan
Presidential Foundation and Library
preserves the legacy of the nation's 40th
president and encourages public interest
in his many contributions to U.S. history.

Ronald W. Reagan Museum and Peace
Garden at Eureka College
Eureka College

300 East College Avenue
Eureka, IL 61530
(309) 467-6382
Web site: http://reagan.eureka.edu/lead
    _applied/museum.htm
The Ronald W. Reagan Museum and Peace
    Garden at Eureka College is home to
    a variety of items and exhibits related
    to Reagan's days as a student at Eureka
    College, his acting career, and time in
    office as both governor and president.

WEB SITES

Due to the changing nature of Internet links,
Rosen Educational Services has developed an
online list of Web sites related to the subject
of this book. This site is updated regularly.
Please use this link to access the list:

http://www.rosenlinks.com/pppl/ronrea

For Further Reading

Benson, Michael. *Ronald Reagan* (Lerner, 2004).

Burgan, Michael. *Ronald Reagan* (DK, 2011).

Doherty, Kieran. *Ronald Reagan: America's 40th President* (Children's, 2005).

Johnson, Darv. *The Reagan Years* (Lucent, 2000).

Kent, Zachary. *Ronald Reagan* (Children's, 1989).

Lawson, Don. *America Held Hostage: The Iran Hostage Crisis and the Iran-Contra Affair* (Franklin Watts, 1991).

Morris, Jeffrey. *The Reagan Way* (Lerner, 1996).

Reagan, Ronald. *An American Life* (Simon & Schuster, 1990).

Schlesinger, A.M. *The Election of 1980 and the Administration of Ronald Reagan* (Mason Crest, 2003).

Sutherland, James. *Ronald Reagan: A Twentieth-Century Life* (Viking, 2008).

Wagner, Heather Lehr. *Ronald Reagan* (Chelsea House, 2004).

Young, J.C. *Great Communicator: The Story of Ronald Reagan* (Morgan Reynolds, 2003).

Index